Writing Handbook

GRADE

1

Houghton Mifflin Harcourt

Contents

Contents

How to Use This Book

This handbook will help you write. It will give you ideas. It will also help you share your ideas.

First, you will read about how to write. Then you will practice writing. Have fun using this book!

Purposes for Writing

Before you write, think about why you are writing. This is your **purpose**.

● **To Inform**

Tell facts. Share what you have learned about a topic.

● **To Explain**

Tell how to do something or how something works.

● **To Narrate**

Share a story. It can be something that really happened or made-up.

● **To Persuade**

Tell your opinion. Give reasons why others should agree with you.

Understanding Task, Audience, and Purpose (TAP)

Your **audience** is who you write for. Are you writing to a friend or a teacher?

Your **task** is what you write. Do you want to write a story or a report?

You can call your task, audience, and purpose your **TAP**.

Think:

Task: <u>What</u> am I writing?

Audience: <u>Who</u> am I writing for?

Purpose: <u>Why</u> am I writing?

The Writing Process

After you think about your TAP, use these five stages to write.

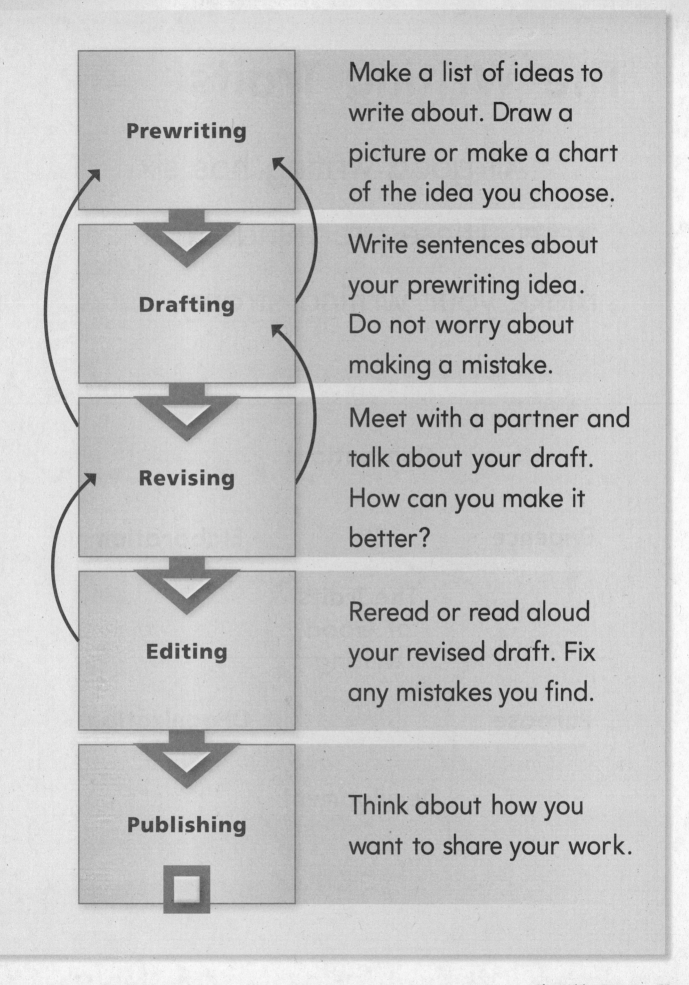

Prewriting

Make a list of ideas to write about. Draw a picture or make a chart of the idea you choose.

Drafting

Write sentences about your prewriting idea. Do not worry about making a mistake.

Revising

Meet with a partner and talk about your draft. How can you make it better?

Editing

Reread or read aloud your revised draft. Fix any mistakes you find.

Publishing

Think about how you want to share your work.

The Writing Traits

All good writing has six traits. These are things that make your writing strong.

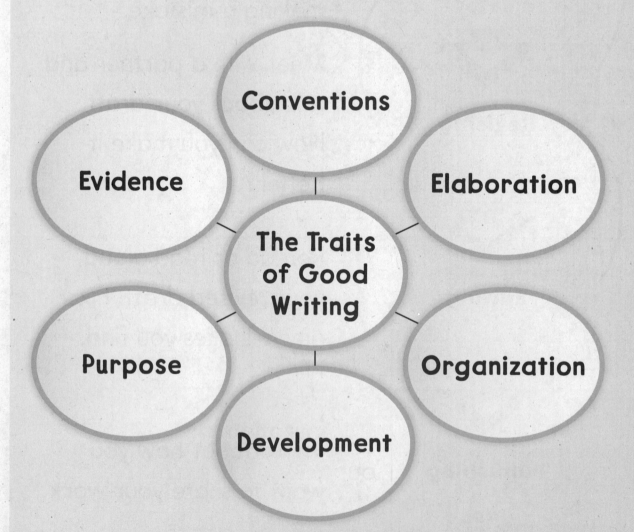

Traits Checklist

When you write, ask these questions.

☑ **Evidence**	Do I have enough details and examples?
☑ **Organization**	Are my words and sentences in an order that makes sense?
☑ **Purpose**	Is my reason for writing clear?
☑ **Elaboration**	Did I choose the best words?
☑ **Development**	Did I tell a good story?
☑ **Conventions**	Are my spelling, grammar, capitalization, and punctuation correct?

Labels

A **label** names an object. It tells what something is or what it looks like.

✏ Parts of a Label

- A label can be one word such as <u>chair</u> or <u>book</u>.
- A label can be more than one word such as <u>red chair</u> or <u>big book</u>.

Follow your teacher's directions.

We Do
1

You Do
2 Draw a picture.

Label three objects in it.

Captions

A **caption** tells about a picture.

Parts of a Caption

- A few words or a sentence about a picture
- Details about what a picture shows

Here is a bench at the park.

Follow your teacher's directions.

1 The family _____

_____

_____

_____ .

2 Use your plan. Write a caption. You can write about a place to visit with your family.

Sentences

A **sentence** gives information. It is a group of words that tells who or what does something.

Parts of a Sentence

- A sentence starts with a capital letter.
- A sentence ends with an end mark.

We play outside.

Jay and Anne run fast.

Pat rides a bike.

Name _____

Follow your teacher's directions.

1 The girl _____

_____

_____.

2 The boy _____

_____

_____.

3 Use your plan. Write a sentence.
Tell what you do at school.

Class Story

A **class story** is a story we write as a class. It can tell about something that really happened. It can describe people and things.

Parts of a Class Story

- Events that are told in complete sentences
- Sentences that include interesting details

The Hike

Our class went for a hike. We climbed up a tall hill. We could see a big lake. The hike made us tired. But we had fun anyway.

Name _____

Follow your teacher's directions.

1 Our class went to the market.

_____

- - - - - - - - - - - - - - - - - - -

We _____

_____

- - - - - - - - - - - - - - - - - - -

_____.

_____

- - - - - - - - - - - - - - - - - - -

We also _____

_____

- - - - - - - - - - - - - - - - - - -

_____.

_____

- - - - - - - - - - - - - - - - - - -

We _____

_____

- - - - - - - - - - - - - - - - - - -

_____.

 2 Think of a detail you could add to the
class story. Write a sentence about it.

Class Story

A **class story** is written together by the class and the teacher.

✏️ Parts of a Class Story

- Sentences that tell events in time order
- Words that describe
- An ending to the story

> Our class went to visit a farm. **First**, we saw five cows. **Next**, we got to feed the red hens. **Last**, we all went for a ride in a big wagon. We had a fun day at the farm.

Name _____

Follow your teacher's directions.

1 Our class went to the zoo.

_____
- -

First, _____

_____
- -
_____.

_____
- -

Then _____

_____
- -
_____.

- -

Later, _____

_____
- -
_____.

2 Think of another event you could add to the class story. Write a sentence about it.

Sentences That Describe

Sentences that describe work together to tell how something looks, sounds, smells, tastes, or feels. Describing words are called adjectives.

Parts of Sentences That Describe

- Details that tell how something looks, sounds, smells, tastes, or feels
- Sentences that tell about just one thing

The Woods

The leaves are soft and green.

The trees feel very bumpy.

I hear loud buzzing.

The air smells fresh.

Follow your teacher's directions.

1 The buildings _____

_____

- -

_____ .

The streets _____

_____

- -

_____ .

The people _____

_____

- -

_____ .

2 Use your plan. Write sentences that describe. You can tell about a place you like to visit.

Poetry

A **poem** is a group of words put together in a special way. A poem can be about a thing or a feeling.

Parts of a Poem

- Interesting words about the topic
- Some words that may rhyme

The Cat

I would like to see a cat

with black stripes in its <u>fur</u>.

I would like to pet the cat

to hear its low, soft <u>purr</u>.

Follow your teacher's directions.

1 I would like to see _____

_____

_____

_____

_____.

I would like to _____

_____

_____

_____

_____.

2 Use your plan. Write a poem. You can write about a favorite animal.

Thank-You Note

A **thank-you note** thanks someone for a favor or a gift.

✏ Parts of a Thank-You Note

- A date, greeting, closing, and your name
- A sentence that tells what you are thanking someone for
- Details that tell your feelings

March 1, 2013

Dear Grandpa,

　　Thank you for the ant farm. It is a great gift! I like to see the ants work. They are so busy.

　　　　　　Love,

　　　　　　Eli

Follow your teacher's directions.

We Do 1

_____

- - - - - - - - - - - - - - - - - - - -

_____

- - - - - - - - - - - - - - - - - - - -

_____

- - - - - - - - - - - - - - - - - - - -

Dear _____,

_____

- - - - - - - - - - - - - - - - - - - -

Thank you for _____

_____

- - - - - - - - - - - - - - - - - - - -

I like _____

_____

- - - - - - - - - - - - - - - - - - - -

_____

Your friend,

_____

- - - - - - - - - - - - - - - - - - - -

_____

You Do 2 Write a thank-you note to a friend or family member.

Description: Prewriting

A **description** can tell how something looks. The writer helps the reader picture a thing in his or her mind.

✏ Parts of a Description

- The topic sentence tells what the description is about.
- Detail sentences use adjectives that tell size, shape, color, or number.

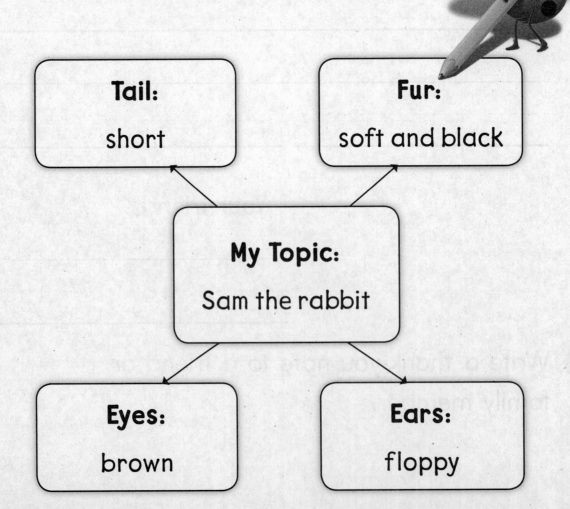

Tail:

short

Fur:

soft and black

My Topic:

Sam the rabbit

Eyes:

brown

Ears:

floppy

Name _____

Follow your teacher's directions.

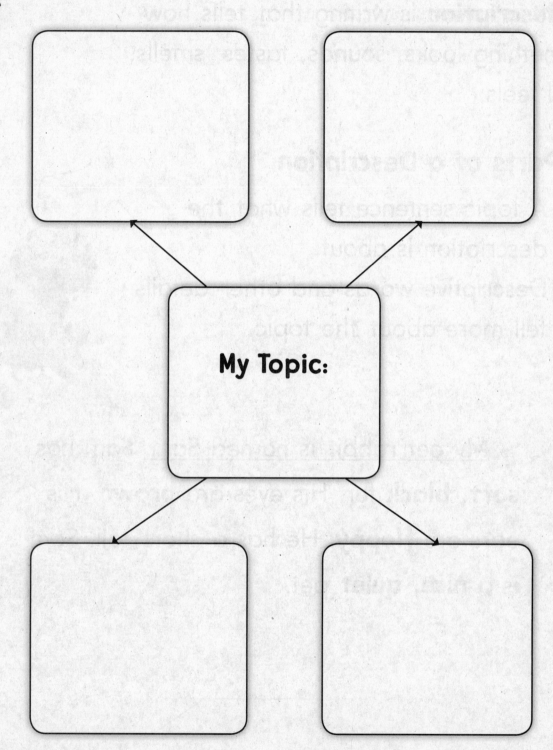

My Topic:

 Use your plan to write about your favorite animal.

Description: Drafting/Revising

A **description** is writing that tells how something looks, sounds, tastes, smells, and feels.

Parts of a Description

- A topic sentence tells what the description is about.
- Descriptive words and other details tell more about the topic.

My pet rabbit is named Sam. Sam has **soft**, **black** fur. His eyes are **brown**. His ears are **floppy**. He has a short tail. Sam is a **nice**, **quiet** pet.

Follow your teacher's directions.

We Do

1 My favorite animal is

_____

- -

_____.

_____

- -

It looks _____

_____

- -

_____.

_____

- -

It is _____.

_____

- -

It has _____

_____

- -

_____.

You Do

2 Use your plan to write a description. If you like, write about a pet you have or would like to have.

Sentences That Inform

Sentences that inform work together to tell facts, or information that is true. Writers use sentences that inform to share what they know.

Parts of Sentences That Inform

- A topic sentence that tells what all the sentences are about
- Detail sentences that tell facts, not opinions
- Some details that describe how something happens

Cows

Cows are big animals on farms.

They walk very slowly.

Cows lie quietly in the grass.

They flick their tails quickly to push away flies.

Name _____

Follow your teacher's directions.

We Do

1 A horse _____

_____

_____ .

It can _____

_____

_____ .

It _____

_____

_____ .

You Do

2 Use your plan. Write sentences that inform. You can write about the animal you chose.

Instructions

Instructions tell how to do or make something.

Parts of Instructions

- Things you need
- Steps to follow in order
- Time-order words such as <u>first</u> and <u>next</u>

Making a Drum

Here is how to make a drum. **First**, get an empty can. **Next**, lay paper over the top. **Then** put a rubber band around the can and the paper. **Last**, get two sticks and play.

Follow your teacher's directions.

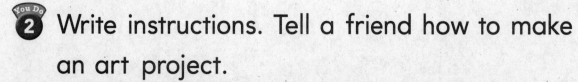

1 Here is how to _____.

_____

First, _____

_____

_____

Next, _____

_____

_____

Last, _____

_____

_____

2 Write instructions. Tell a friend how to make an art project.

Sentences That Inform

Sentences that inform tell facts about the world. Facts are things that are true.

Parts of Sentences That Inform

- A topic sentence tells what all of the sentences are about.
- Detail sentences tell facts, not opinions.
- All of the sentences are about one main idea.

All About Trees

Trees are big plants.

Leaves grow on trees.

There are lots of trees in the forest.

Birds build their nests in trees.

Follow your teacher's directions.

We Do

1 Ducks are _____

_____

_____

_____.

A duck can _____

_____

_____

_____.

Ducks _____

_____

_____

_____.

You Do

2 Use your plan. Write sentences that inform. You can write about a season you like.

Report: Prewriting

A **report** tells facts about a topic. When people write reports, they can find the facts they need in books.

Parts of a Report

- The topic sentence tells what the report is about.
- Detail sentences give facts about the topic.
- Writers do research to find facts about a topic.

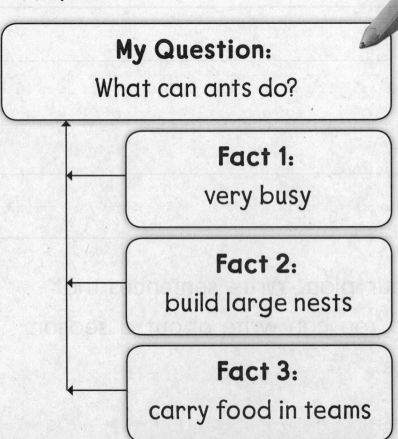

My Question:
What can ants do?

Fact 1:
very busy

Fact 2:
build large nests

Fact 3:
carry food in teams

Follow your teacher's directions.

1

My Question:

Fact 1:

Fact 2:

Fact 3:

2 Use your plan to write about an animal
you know about.

Report: Drafting/Revising

A **report** gives facts about a topic. You write the facts in your own words.

✏️ Parts of a Report

- A topic sentence tells what the report is about.
- Detail sentences tell the facts.
- A closing ties ideas together.

Ants

Ants are busy little animals. One thing ants do is build large nests. Another thing they do is carry food in teams. Ants work like this all over the world!

Follow your teacher's directions.

1 (We Do)

_____

- -

_____ are animals

_____

- -

that _____ .

_____

- -

One thing _____

_____

- -

_____ .

_____

- -

Another thing _____

_____

- -

_____ .

2 (You Do) Use your plan. Write a report. Tell about an animal you know about.

Sentences About Yourself

A **sentence about yourself** tells a true story about you. It uses the words I or me.

✏ Parts of a Sentence About Yourself

- A topic sentence tells the main idea.
- Detail sentences tell what happened.
- Some details tell who or what.

At the Lake

I went swimming at the lake last week.

The water was freezing cold!

Mom wrapped me in a warm towel when I got out.

Follow your teacher's directions.

1 I went _____
_____
_____ .

It was _____
_____
_____ .

I _____
_____
_____ .

2 Use your plan. Write sentences about yourself. If you like, write about nature.

Sentences About Yourself

A **sentence about yourself** tells about something real that happened to you. It has the words <u>I</u>, <u>me</u>, or <u>we</u>.

Parts of a Sentence About Yourself

- A topic sentence tells what all the sentences will be about.
- Detail sentences tell what happened and in what order.
- Details may tell where or when things happened.

My Cousins

Yesterday **I** went to my cousin's house.

First, **we** put on a puppet show.

After that, **we** played football in the park.

Name _____

Follow your teacher's directions.

_____

We Do

1 My family _____

_____

_____ .

First, we _____

_____

_____ .

Later, _____

_____

_____ .

You Do

2 Use your plan. Write sentences about yourself. You can write about something you like to do.

Friendly Letter

A **friendly letter** is written to another person.

Parts of a Letter

- The **date**
- A **greeting** to the person the letter is for
- A **body** that tells what you want to say
- A **closing** and **your name**

April 19, 2012

Dear Ben,

    I am at camp. I just made a drum. I made it from a tin can.

                  Your pal,

                  Jon

Follow your teacher's directions.

1 (We Do)

_____

- -

_____

_____

- -

Dear _____,

_____

- -

_____

_____

- -

_____

_____

- -

_____

Your friend,

_____

- -

_____

2 (You Do) Use your plan, or make a new one.
Write a letter about a trip.

Personal Narrative: Prewriting

A **personal narrative** tells a true story about the author. It uses the words <u>I</u> or <u>me</u>.

Parts of a Personal Narrative

- It tells events in the order they happened.
- It uses time order words like <u>first</u>, <u>next</u>, <u>soon</u>, and <u>later</u>.

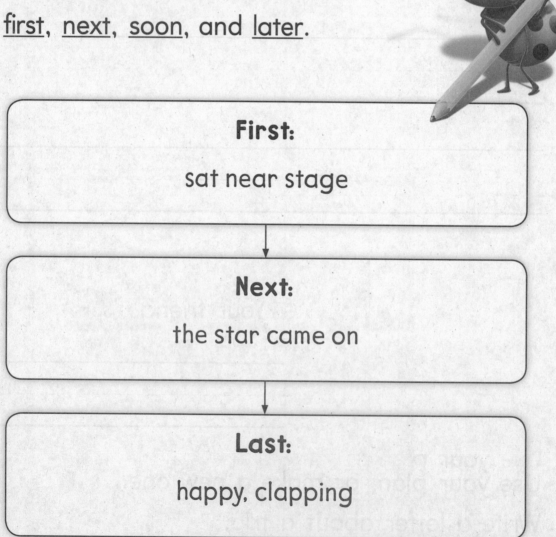

First:

sat near stage

Next:

the star came on

Last:

happy, clapping

Follow your teacher's directions.

1

First:

Next:

Last:

2 Use your plan to write about
a place you went.

Personal Narrative: Drafting/Revising

A **personal narrative** is a true story about something you did.

✏ Parts of a Personal Narrative

- Sentences tell what you did in time order.
- Sentences use words like <u>I</u>, <u>me</u>, or <u>we</u>.
- An ending ties ideas together.

My family went to a play. **First**, we sat down close to the stage. **Then** the star of the show walked on stage. He wore a big red hat. He sang many funny songs. **At the end**, we felt happy. We stood and clapped.

Follow your teacher's directions.

1 I went on a fun trip to _____

_____

First, _____

_____

_____.

Then _____

_____

_____.

At the end, _____

_____

_____.

2 Use your plan. Write a personal narrative. If you like, write what you did with your family.

Story Sentences

Story sentences show us how characters think and feel. **Dialogue** can tell the exact words characters say.

Parts of Dialogue Story Sentences

- They tell the exact words that the characters say.
- The characters are make-believe.
- Quotation marks tell where the characters start and stop talking.

Here Comes the Train!

Zoe looked along the train tracks.

"I see the train!" she said.

The train slid to a stop at the station.

"We're going for a train ride!"

Zoe's brother Sam shouted.

Name _____

Follow your teacher's directions.

1 Allie and Jane _____

_____

_____

_____

"Look at _____

_____

_____," said Allie.

"It is _____," said Jane.

2 Use your plan. Write story sentences. If you like, write about the book you read.

Story Sentences

Story sentences tell what make-believe characters say and do.

Parts of Story Sentences

- The characters are make-believe.
- Details tell the events in order.
- Vivid verbs tell what the characters do.

The Geese

Two geese were swimming in the river.

Then they spotted some bread crumbs in the water.

The geese swallowed the crumbs.

After that, they paddled home and fell asleep.

Follow your teacher's directions.

We Do
1 Some _____

_____

_____

First, _____

_____

_____

Then _____

_____

_____

You Do
2 Use your plan. Write story sentences. You can write about your favorite animal.

Story Summary

A **story summary** tells what happens in a story. You write the summary in your own words.

Parts of a Story Summary

- Sentences tell the parts of a story in the order they happen.
- Sentences tell only the most important parts.

Whistle for Willie

First, Peter wanted to whistle. **Next**, he tried hard, but no whistle came out. **At last**, Peter tried again and he whistled!

Name _____

Follow your teacher's directions.

We Do 1

_____

_____

_____

First, _____

_____

_____

Next, _____

_____

_____

At last, _____

_____

_____

You Do 2 Use your plan, or make a new one.

Write a summary about a story you like.

Story: Prewriting

A **story** tells something that is made-up.
It comes from the author's imagination.

Parts of a Story

- The beginning introduces the characters.
- The middle tells about a problem.
- The end tells how the characters solve the problem.

Characters	Setting
2 girls Jane and Meg	school

Plot

Beginning:

new watch
bring it to school

Middle:

watch gets lost (problem)
girls look for it

End:

found in book bag

Name _____

Follow your teacher's directions.

Characters	Setting

Plot

Beginning:

Middle:

End:

 Use your plan to write a new story.

Story: Drafting/Revising

A **story** tells what happens to the characters in it.

Parts of a Story

- A title
- Sentences that tell what happens at the beginning, in the middle, and at the end
- A problem that the characters solve

Jane's New Watch

Jane got a new watch. **First**, she wore it to school. **Then** she lost the watch. Jane asked her friend Meg to help. **At last**, Jane and Meg found the watch. It was in Jane's book bag!

Follow your teacher's directions.

We Do 1

_____

- -

_____

- -

_____

First, _____

- -

_____ .

Then _____

- -

_____ .

At last, _____ .

You Do 2 Use your plan. Write a new story.

Opinion Sentences

Opinion sentences tell something you believe. They can show your strong feelings about a topic.

Parts of Opinion Sentences

- The topic sentence tells your opinion, or what you think.
- Detail sentences tell the reasons for your opinion.
- An exclamation shows that you feel strongly about something.

Basketball

Basketball is my favorite sport!

You have to run fast and play hard in a basketball game.

It feels great when you score some points for your team!

Follow your teacher's directions.

1 My favorite _____

_____

_____ .

I like _____ .

It is great when _____

_____

_____ .

2 Use your plan. Write opinion sentences.
You can write about your favorite thing
to do.

Opinion Sentences

Opinion sentences tell something you think. You can use the word <u>because</u> to explain your reasons.

Parts of Opinion Sentences

- The topic sentence gives your opinion, or what you believe.
- Detail sentences tell the reasons for your opinion.
- The word <u>because</u> tells that you are about to give a reason.

My Garden

I love spending time in my garden!

It is fun **because** I get to dig lots of holes.

It also feels good to help the plants get bigger.

Follow your teacher's directions.

We Do 1 I like _____
_____
_____
_____.

It is fun _____
_____
_____
_____.

I also like _____.

You Do 2 Use your plan. Write opinion sentences. Write about something you learned how to do.

Opinion Sentences

Opinion sentences tell what you believe. They give reasons why you have that opinion.

✏ Parts of Opinion Sentences

- The topic sentence tells your opinion, or what you think.
- Detail sentences tell the reasons for your opinion.
- Exact words make the ideas clear.

At the Circus

We saw the best circus ever!

One funny part was when a lot of clowns hopped out of a tiny car.

I loved the dancer's blue dress because it was so sparkly.

Follow your teacher's directions.

1 The zoo _____

_____

_____

I saw _____

_____

_____

The _____

_____

_____

2 Use your plan. Write opinion sentences.
If you like, you can write about the story
you read.

Opinion Paragraph: Prewriting

An **opinion paragraph** is a group of sentences about one feeling or belief.

Parts of an Opinion Paragraph

- The topic sentence tells your opinion, or what you think.
- Detail sentences give reasons and examples.
- The closing sentence retells your opinion using different words.

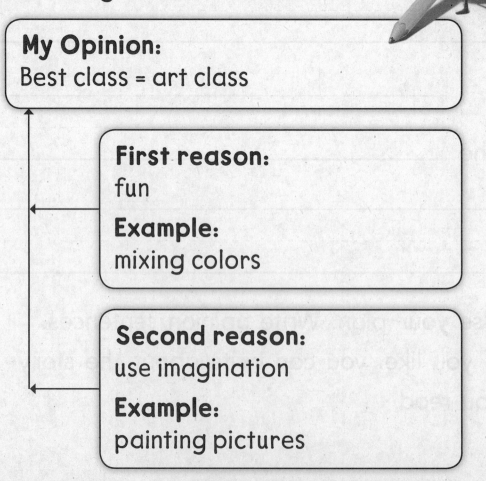

My Opinion:
Best class = art class

First reason:
fun

Example:
mixing colors

Second reason:
use imagination

Example:
painting pictures

Name _____

Follow your teacher's directions.

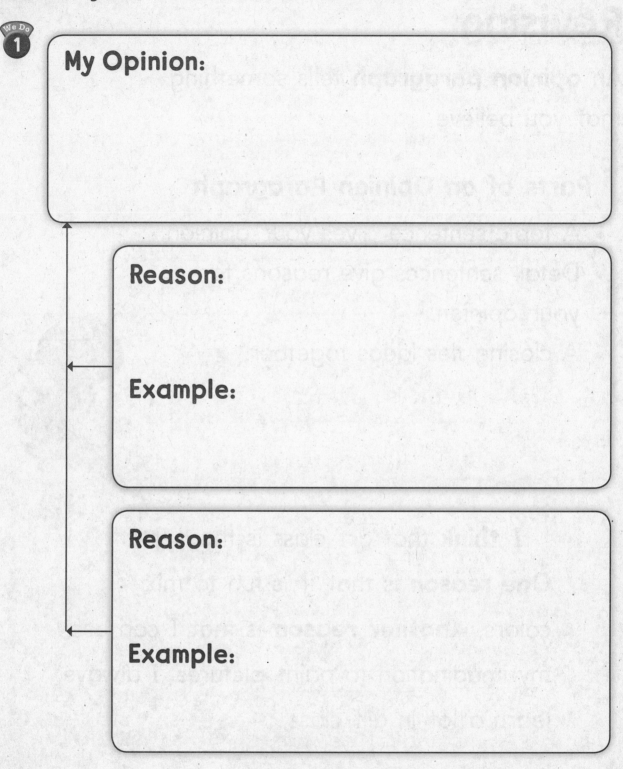

1

My Opinion:

Reason:

Example:

Reason:

Example:

2 Use your plan to write about an opinion you have.

Opinion Paragraph: Drafting/Revising

An **opinion paragraph** tells something that you believe.

Parts of an Opinion Paragraph

- A topic sentence gives your opinion.
- Detail sentences give reasons for your opinion.
- A closing ties ideas together.

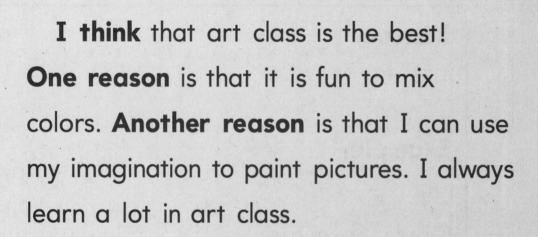

I think that art class is the best! **One reason** is that it is fun to mix colors. **Another reason** is that I can use my imagination to paint pictures. I always learn a lot in art class.

Follow your teacher's directions.

We Do

1 I think _____

_____

_____ .

One reason is _____

_____

_____ .

Another reason is _____

_____

_____ .

You Do

2 Use your plan. Write sentences to tell your opinion.

Prewriting

The five stages of writing are prewriting, drafting, revising, editing, and publishing. This lesson tells about **prewriting.**

Parts of Prewriting

- List ideas to write about.
- Choose the idea you like best.
- Fill in a word web.

Ideas

- my trip to the zoo
- letter to Grandma
- poem about a whale

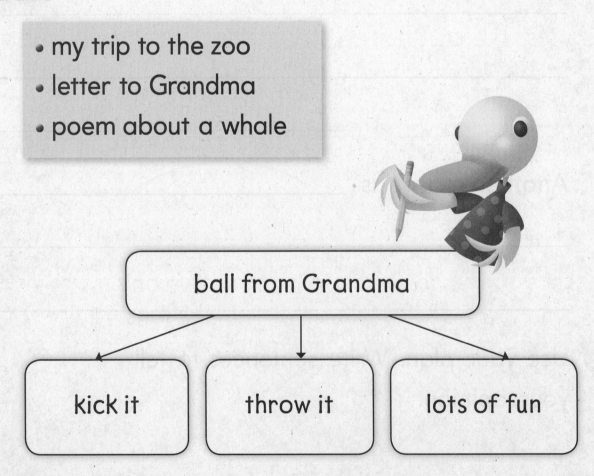

ball from Grandma

kick it   throw it   lots of fun

There are more organizers you can use to help fill out your ideas. Use them to plan your writing.

Flow Chart

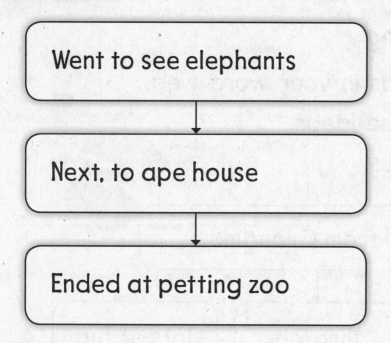

Went to see elephants

↓

Next, to ape house

↓

Ended at petting zoo

Venn Diagram to Compare and Contrast

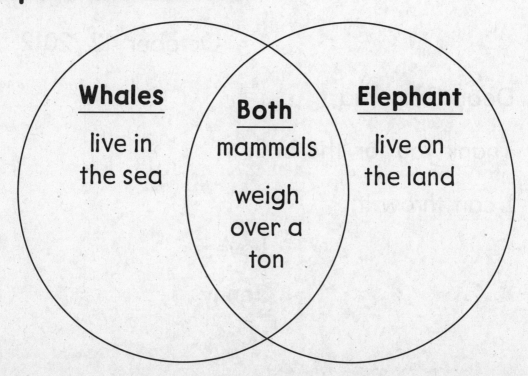

Whales
live in the sea

Both
mammals

weigh over a ton

Elephant
live on the land

Drafting

When you **draft,** you use full sentences to write what you planned.

✏ Parts of Drafting

- Look at the ideas in your word web.
- Write about these ideas.
- Use full sentences.

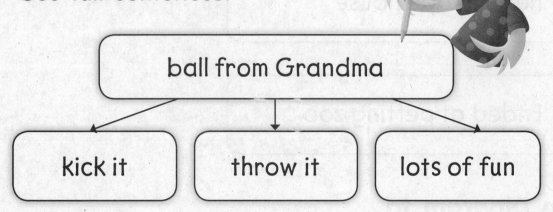

ball from Grandma

kick it   throw it   lots of fun

October 12, 2012

Dear Grandma,

Thank you for the ball.

I can throw it.

Love,

Jenny

Here is how Ben used his plan. He wrote sentences about a book from his friend Allie.

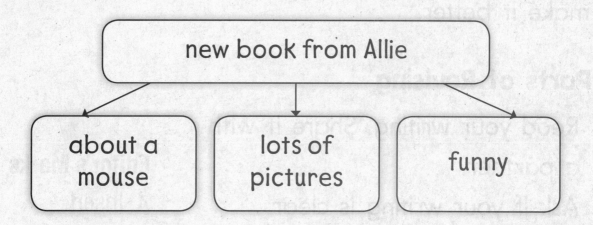

Allie gave me a book.

The book is about a mouse.

It has lots of pictures.

I think it is very funny.

Revising

When you **revise**, you change your writing to make it better.

Parts of Revising

- Read your writing. Share it with a partner.
- Ask if your writing is clear.
- Make your writing better.
- Use editor's marks.

Editor's Marks

∧ Insert.

⸜ Delete.

⊙ Make a period.

October 12, 2012

Dear Grandma,

soccer

Thank you for the ∧ ball.

It is fun to throw it and kick it with my

I can throw it. ⸜ friends.

∧

Love,

Jenny

Here is how Ben revised his writing.

First, he read his draft to a friend.
Next, he listened. His friend asked
questions.
Last, Ben changed his writing. He changed
words and sentences.

Allie gave me a new book.

The book is about a mouse.

It has lots of funny pictures.

I laughed a lot.
I think it is very funny.

Editing

When you **edit**, you fix mistakes in your writing.

✏ Parts of Editing

- Make sure your spelling is correct.
- Check that your sentences have end marks.
- Put capital letters where they belong.

March 15, 2012

Dear Arlo,

T̲hank you for the baseball bat.

                    far
I̲ can hit very for with it.

                 size
It is a good sise for me.

Your friend,

Peter

Publishing

When you **publish** your writing, you share it. You make it look as good as you can.

Parts of Publishing

- Make a clean copy.
- Maybe draw a picture or use computer art to go with it.
- Share your work.

Dear Grandma,

Thank you for the soccer ball.

It is fun to throw it and kick it with my friends.

Love,

Jenny

Evidence

Before you write, think of **ideas.**

Ideas

- Think about what you will write.
- Draw pictures, write lists, or make webs.

Informative Writing

Think of topics for a report. Make a list of details about your topic.

Hermit Crabs

live in shells they find

ten legs

eat plants

good pets

Informative Writing

Think of how to do something. Write words about the steps in order.

Bathing a Dog

1. Fill a bathtub with water.

2. With an adult, put the dog in the tub.

3. Wet the dog's fur.

4. Wash the dog's fur with shampoo.

5. Take the dog out of the tub, and dry its fur.

Persuasive Writing

Think of an opinion. Make a list of reasons.

Eat More Vegetables!

1. vitamins

2. help you grow strong

3. taste good

Organization

Organization is when you put your ideas in order.

✏ Organization

- Think of a good beginning.
- Make a plan.
- Put your ideas in order.

Narrative Writing

Tell about something that happened to you. Put your ideas in the order they happened.

Our class went to the fire station.

We sat in the fire truck.

We put on boots and helmets.

Informative Writing

Write a topic sentence. Write facts about the topic.

> The sun is the center of the solar system.
>
> It is close to the Earth.
>
> It keeps us warm.
>
> All the planets turn around the sun.

Persuasive Writing

Tell your opinion. List your reasons. One way is to put the most important reason last.

> Baseball is the best sport.
>
> Games are very exciting.
>
> It is a fun sport to play and a fun sport to watch.
>
> My favorite part is hitting a home run.

Purpose

Purpose is your reason for writing. You can write to tell a story, to inform, to explain, or to persuade.

✏ Purpose

- Think about why you are writing.
- Carefully choose words.
- Grab your reader's attention at the beginning.
- End your writing in an interesting way.

Juicy oranges are my favorite fruit.

They make me think of sunshine.

I love to eat oranges in the summer.

The sticky juice drips all over my fingers.

That's why you should like juicy oranges, too!

Elaboration

When you **write**, think about the words
you use.

Word Choice

- Use exact words.
- Use words that describe. Help make
  a picture in the reader's mind.

I share a <u>warm</u> pie with my friends.

We cut it into <u>six</u> pieces.

The pie has a <u>tasty</u> crust.

It has <u>sweet</u> apples inside.

Development

When you write a story, add details that tell about the characters, setting, and the events.

✏ Development

- Choose words that help readers picture where the story takes place.
- Add details that give information about who the story is about.
- Keep readers interested in what is happening in the story by adding intersting details.

It was a dark, stormy night. Jimmy and his mom were home alone watching a movie. Then there was a loud clap of thunder. Everything in the house shook. The lights went out. In a flash, Jimmy was in his mom's arms.

Make every sentence in your story count.

- Add time-order words.
- Make your sentences fun to read.
- Use statements and questions.

Jimmy wondered if his mom was as scared as he was. One glance at her face told him she was. What were they going to do? First his mom told Jimmy to be brave. As they went to get a flashlight, the lights came back on. It was still rainy and very windy outside. Inside Jimmy and his mom were once again cozy!

Conventions

After you write, check for mistakes.

Conventions

- Check for spelling.
- Check for capital letters.
- Check for correct end marks.

Dear Megan,

    I went to the ~~ise~~ ^ice^ rink. ~~have~~ ^Have^ you

ever been there? You can skate and do

spins ^⊙^

                Your friend,
                Susana

Singular and Plural Nouns

A singular noun names one. A plural noun names more than one and ends in an s.

Wrong Way	Right Way
We put everything in box.	We put everything in boxes.

Complete Sentences

A complete sentence begins with a capital letter and ends with a period.

Wrong Way	Right Way
one day he ran a race	One day he ran a race.

Correct Use of I and me

I is always in the subject of a sentence.

Wrong Way	Right Way
Erin and me went home.	Erin and I went home.

Describing Words with er and est

Some describing words tell how things are different.

Wrong Way	Right Way
A baseball is small than a basketball.	A baseball is smaller than a basketball.

Using the Computer

Use a **computer** to find information about your topic on the Internet.

✏ Using the Computer

- Go to a web page that has information about your topic.
- Take notes to help you remember.

| File | Edit | View | Favorites | Tools | Help |

Address http://www.---.org

ALL ABOUT POLAR BEARS

HOME
CONTACT
ABOUT US
NEWS

Polar bears live in a cold place called the Arctic. They have thick white fur that keeps them warm. They are good swimmers.

Polar bears

- live in the Arctic

- have thick white fur

- good at swimming

Here is another example.

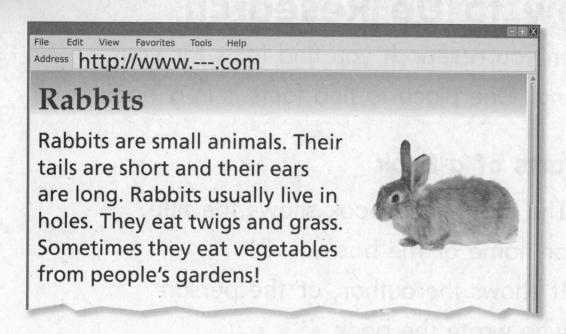

File   Edit   View   Favorites   Tools   Help

Address http://www.---.com

Rabbits

Rabbits are small animals. Their tails are short and their ears are long. Rabbits usually live in holes. They eat twigs and grass. Sometimes they eat vegetables from people's gardens!

Rabbits

- short tails, long ears

- live in holes

- eat twigs, grass, and vegetables

How to Do Research

When you **research** you find facts for your writing. One place to find facts is in a book.

Parts of a Book

- The cover of a book shows the title, or name of the book.
- It shows the author, or the person who wrote the book.
- It also shows the illustrator, or person who made the pictures.

Cover

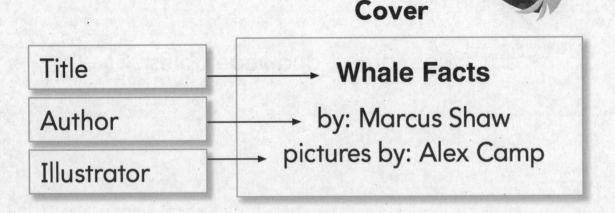

Title	→	**Whale Facts**
Author	→	by: Marcus Shaw
Illustrator	→	pictures by: Alex Camp

Table of Contents

This page shows page numbers where you can find information in a book.

Contents

Index

These pages show topics and page numbers. The topics are shown in ABC order.

Checklists and Rubrics

Use this list to check your writing. Make sure you have done everything on the list.

✏ How to Use a Checklist

- Read the checklist.
- Check your writing.
- After you check, fix your writing.
- After you fix, go back and check the list. Make sure you fixed all mistakes.

√ My writing is on topic.

√ My writing has facts or details.

√ My writing has a beginning and an ending.

√ Ideas are in order.

√ Words are spelled correctly.

√ Sentences and names start with capital letters.

√ Sentences have correct end marks.